VASECTOMANIA

AKRON ... ES IN POETRY

AKRON SERIES IN POETRY
Mary Biddinger, Editor

Matthew Guenette, *Vasectomania*

Sandra Simonds, *Further Problems with Pleasure*

Leslie Harrison, *The Book of Endings*

Emilia Phillips, *Groundspeed*

Philip Metres, *Pictures at an Exhibition: A Petersburg Album*

Jennifer Moore, *The Veronica Maneuver*

Brittany Cavallaro, *Girl-King*

Oliver de la Paz, *Post Subject: A Fable*

John Repp, *Fat Jersey Blues*

Emilia Phillips, *Signaletics*

Seth Abramson, *Thievery*

Steve Kistulentz, *Little Black Daydream*

Jason Bredle, *Carnival*

Emily Rosko, *Prop Rockery*

Alison Pelegrin, *Hurricane Party*

Matthew Guenette, *American Busboy*

Joshua Harmon, *Le Spleen de Poughkeepsie*

David Dodd Lee, *Orphan, Indiana*

Sarah Perrier, *Nothing Fatal*

Oliver de la Paz, *Requiem for the Orchard*

Rachel Dilworth, *The Wild Rose Asylum*

John Minczeski, *A Letter to Serafin*

John Gallaher, *Map of the Folded World*

Heather Derr-Smith, *The Bride Minaret*

William Greenway, *Everywhere at Once*

Brian Brodeur, *Other Latitudes*

Titles published since 2008.
For a complete listing of titles published in the series,
go to www.uakron.edu/uapress/poetry.

VASECTOMANIA

MATTHEW GUENETTE

The University of Akron Press
Akron, Ohio

Copyright © 2017 by The University of Akron Press
All rights reserved · First Edition 2017 · Manufactured in the United States of America.
All inquiries and permission requests should be addressed to the publisher,
The University of Akron Press, Akron, Ohio 44325-1703.

ISBN: 978-1-629220-89-5 (paper)
ISBN: 978-1-629220-90-1 (ePDF)
ISBN: 978-1-629220-91-8 (ePub)

A catalog record for this title is available from the Library of Congress.

∞The paper used in this publication meets the minimum requirements of ANSI/NISO z39.48–1992 (Permanence of Paper).

Cover: Photo by Matthew Guenette. Cover design by Tyler Krusinski.

Vasectomania was designed and typeset in Mrs. Eaves, with Univers display, by Amy Freels and printed on sixty-pound natural and bound by Bookmasters of Ashland, Ohio.

Contents

III. Dear Kids...

parenting is a contingency
of time, activities,

and anthropomorphized animals
having petty arguments

about who can stack
the most apples on their heads

I: A Bag of Frozen Peas...

Zero Thoughts of You

When the kids were raised to be ditched for boyfriends, ditched for contractors and dope dealers, when the weirdo with the mullet dunked chicken nuggets in chocolate milk, when he threw piss balloons at the school bus just doing whatever felt good, when what we wished for would depend on our definition of "is," when we thought the toilet flushed funny, or pet goats were funny, or it was funny to hit your head on a door, when the uncle who whizzed on an electric fence called me the idiot, when I helped an old lady across the street that time, when the gun factory where everyone's dad or uncle worked seemed rhetorical, when even its exceedingly well-built guns seemed rhetorical, when I knew the rhetoric could tear us apart, when I was dreaming "not me," when I side-eyed the lifted truck and hill-rods in the parking lot whistling at someone's sister, when we used Saran Wrap for the screen door gaps and duct tape for a sorry ass, when I wondered if philosophy made a sound if a mom only cried when no one was around, when I tried not to drown in the current, when the frozen dinners in the freezer were burning, when the frozen peas were a state of mind like highlights or chicken gizzards, when I scored a job at the corner store, when they stuck a price gun in my hand to go and kill the Mello Yello sale, I had zero thoughts of you.

Bastille Day

For the cracker crumbs growing a reef
      beneath the cushions. For the bedtime story
where the three little pigs are classless

idiots and the wolf speaks like a chicken.
      For the grocery cart lickers and dance moves.
For the unbelievable all we get for free.

For the son who slaps himself when happy.
      Why are you doing that, I ask.
Because I'm crazy, he says. For the yelling

      and worry and years of scorekeeping
slowly letting me go. For this breakup is mutual.
      For things that feel easy, all the candy lifted

      from waiting rooms. Don't thank me, commander.
Thank Dr. B's office. For the cheap fireworks,
      for the dirty diapers forgotten on heat vents

      or under beds. For the way we refrain
from eating our young. For knockoffs
      passed off as the real thing. For the conditions

      of unconditional love: listening, for instance,
to "Shake Your Rump to the Funk"
      ten times in a row, knowing when

to quit or to use cartoons to down the kids
      for a quickie. For the times
we thought, is this it? For the times

we transformed ourselves into droids,
        sensitive and overeager, extremely willing
to listen. For turns in the root of each word.

        For telepathy. For the fear that makes us sexy
when it rolls up our sleeves.
        For the imperfect teeth, for the privilege

        of toothpaste and toilet paper. For the slow
reveal. For even the spoons and salt, even the ink
        the kids inked on the wall.

Un-Buddha

The house sitter fucks up
    scooping the box,
        clogs the toilet with a week's worth

of unnecessary, not even funny, unflushed
    flushable litter. J stays calm,
ready for honest effort, while I plunge
    and plunge in a boiling freak-out,

        saying to no one in particular—"Seriously?
           A monkey would know better
           than this!"
    I assassinate

the *I-was-only-trying-to-help* house sitter's character.
    Meanwhile, upstairs,
        the kids can totally hear. I'm aware of this.

        Even before the show is over, I know
this will be a way I'm remembered:
        dad in the basement screaming
        at a toilet,

    dad screaming at a cat box, dad screaming
        at a fat, scuzzy cat. Undignified Dad.
        Unmindful.
Throwing one of his famous, outsized

    and short-lived fits. When they're older,
        grown and out of the house, they'll
        reminisce
    this version of me.

They'll laugh if I'm lucky and for Father' Day
        send me a tie patterned with cats.

A Late-Night Conversation with My Infant Son in a Convenience Store Parking Lot

And my son was like, dad, dad, you're distracted. Bedtime at best is a flimsy referent. An abstraction no more provable than God.... It's less a specific designation and more a knob-&-tube operation....

So I said, okay, sure, but still.... How did parents survive before clocks? Did kids, no matter how overtired and cranky, just stay up till whenever? Is bedtime time itself chained to the meat of things? How far can this metaphor go?

And my son was like, dad, dad, a clock is nothing. All it does is administer your thoughts. For a cranky child, time is a roof that leaks. Rain is a clue....

So I said, sure, maybe, *maybe*. But what if the cranky child *is* the clock? An artery pumping from some supreme bedtime as proof of the divine? And while we're here.... What's up with all those tears? Are they not for want of sleep? And isn't sleep the want of death? And death the want of life?

By then my son's head had rolled toward the window. He might have been dreaming already. I quietly opened the door and slipped into the convenience store. A man in front of me was buying condoms with exact change....

What I wanted were those awful powdered mini-doughnuts. I planned to pop two in my mouth like aspirin, right there at the register.

DIAPER

—after Robert Lax

THE FIRST DIAPER THE SECOND DIAPER THE
THIRD DIAPER THE FOURTH DIAPER THE FIFTH
DIAPER THE SIXTH DIAPER THE SEVENTH
DIAPER THE EIGHTH DIAPER THE NINTH DIAPER
THE TENTH DIAPER THE ELEVENTH DIAPER THE
TWELFTH DIAPER THE HUNDRED & TWENTY-
FIRST DIAPER THE HUNDRED & FORTY-FORTH
DIAPER THE TWO THOUSAND SEVEN HUNDRED
& THIRTY-SEVENTH & A HALF DIAPER THE FIVE
THOUSAND FOUR HUNDRED & SEVENTY-FIFTH
DIAPER DIAPER DIAPERS

On Road Trips

Our family, held together with tape and glue,
        would make for a mighty sex ed video.
               It's impressive how J and I manage
not to crack open our heads on the dash,
                   though it could be amazing
             to see our frustrations poured out there
             sizzling in the heat.
Everyone gets tired of counting sheep;
                       the rest stops
      are filthy and a million miles apart.
When the endless fit our kids pitch cranks up another notch
and Eddie Money's "Two Tickets to Paradise"
           comes on the radio yet again,
      I take the fat rubber band
that dangles from the rear view, load it up around
      my trigger finger and thumb,
         and take myself hostage.

A Bird in the Rafters at Wal-Mart

I took a swing at someone famous.
Except it wasn't someone famous; it was a poster of
someone famous, so the misogynist bastard
still broke my hand.

We would ride out to Breakneck Road
and attempt beautiful things. Push a shopping cart
off a bridge, follow the wisdom
of a preemptive first punch, get wrecked
while someone's sad step-mom
danced in her underwear.

Remember the mud derby? We fell in love
with Joan of Anarchy. We fell in love with Britney
Smears. Those concession stand sandwiches
that would never concede exactly
what they were made of . . .

All these years later I still have nightmares
about murderous hillbillies and chairs
made of duct-tape,
but those dreams end in a rush.

Even my disappointments have been a privilege.

Flemmox

—MAY CAUSE UNCERTAINTY

if you think hard work will get you there; if you get involved; if you do any of these while driving: switch outfits, change diapers, play piano, sew or knit, eat soup, read with both feet up; if you wear backwards; if you foster lost causes; if you continually check the fridge; if you are unwilling to admit it; if you start in the middle; if you hang upside down on the monkey bars; if you refuse to move from the haunted; if you continue to craft the perfect comeback long after the moment has passed; if you steal candy from waiting rooms; if you fake out your shadow; if something in your chest involuntarily spasms; if you anger the mall cops; if you ever thought for one second; if you replace the dead fish without telling; if you open umbrellas indoors, lick frozen poles; if you stole those cat-shaped salt & pepper shakers; if you spin or spun the bottle for seven minutes in heaven; if once you could handle a great many scissors but now, now; if you believe belief and you believe it goes both ways; if you parallax; if you wipe your hands on your pants; if you cannot wait to get home and take them off; if you insist or ever get offended; if you have mountain climbing accidents; if you hang out behind supermarkets or listen to the same song on repeat for days; if you buy knockoffs then try to pass them off; if you feel like a loser for having never dropped acid or had a threesome; if you're not so sure anymore; if you've ever picked your nose or peed in the tub; if snooping through the bathroom cabinets is something you relate to; if you believe after if; if you insist; even if there is a pill for this, or an app, what pent up irresistible untold do you crave?—

Communion

Sometimes you spill beer on the quilt
hand-stitched by French-Canucks.
Sometimes you're the denim tuxedo,
the heart's stomping feet,
so you google variations on "white trash foods,"
get Jerry Springer and Paris Hilton,
Texas and the Carolinas, hipsters rocking
ironic mullets making fun on Reddit

of fried everythings entombed
in busted food pyramids.
Theme parties (posted to Pinterest)
featuring tins of Spam, sausage on sticks,
and Frito pies, make you think

of bored soccer moms.
Or bored soccer dads.
And of course you laugh.
And of course it's not funny.
A tin of Spam tossed like a brick

through your window—
those meals are someone's childhood.
Some of those meals were your childhood.
You think of a casserole, a can of tuna tossed in,
clumps of peas from a frozen bag

you could use to cool a sting. American
as failure or lawn fertilizer, as making out
in a pick-up truck or someone's dad
getting sent home from work.
America can take anything
and remove its soul, arm wrestling with devils
to bring us Freedom Toast.
You think of Velveeta, viscous as glue

in a sweater, and Miracle Whip on a Steak-Umm
for a fast Philly cheese
you could have murdered Caesar with.

For your mother, who never went to college,
who had terrible luck with men and so
raised you on her own, whose shadow even now
grows in your thoughts, it was a matter
of convenience.
When you think of sticky situations

and some politician who has never been there
saying, "Lazy bastard,"
you simmer like a pot of baked beans.
And though you might godfather in the Chef Boyardee
and Chex Mix that goes down like Ritalin,
it's true, these foods that practically raised you
you never intend to feed your kids.

You feel a sadness then like you might have
anthropomorphizing a box of Banquet Chicken
burning past its expiration
at the back of a freezer.
You feel about certain foods how you used to feel
about your kid brother: you could pick on him all day,
but nobody else better try it.
You think of bologna and mustard on white bread

and a side of Bugles, which could be the tin sound
of money or the horn of an uncle's Chevy
where everyone went to get high.
Even a cat will eat Bugles.
Even smoke flies into clarity, even love

with all its weight and pain,
which is why you'll still eat fish sticks, still eat a Twinkie
with that god-knows-what holding it together,
its shelf life like a communion wafer
near to the promise of forever.

Totally Doable

|

The students
        talking about purity rings.
The colleague
        who says, Welcome to the Bible Belt!

        Your friend in another city
who went to the school
        where you teach now
says, that's nothing,
        try *dating* someone
with a purity ring.

You try not to take
their purity personally.

You try not to let
their talk of purity
fill you with impure thoughts.
You try not to feel like a creep.

You imagine the chastity belt must be
the purity ring's cruel uncle.
You feel bad for the boy-and-girlfriends
if they even exist,

pumped through no doubt
with enough juice to run a city.
You're aware of the implications.

        You're unsure if this thinking
makes you an asshole.
        You know the world is rich
with many truths,

but what you want
is something dirty,
to march those coeds into the sun
and tell them it's all a hoax.

You read somewhere that a purity ring
delays the loss of virginity
by about nine months—
the time it takes to lose

two semesters of fun
while waiting for the baby to come.

Then your friend in another city
says when she was a straight-edge teen
she had to sign a Code of Conduct.
Among its demands—

One may not sit on a surface
with a member of the opposite sex
unless both parties have
at least one foot on the floor.

You both agree,
that still would be totally doable.

Is that the good news or the bad?
Then your friend in another city
tells you a story
about a guy she knew
who swallowed his girlfriend's purity ring

while they fucked in a car.
I like to think of them, she says,
fishing it out from his shit.

A Bag of Frozen Peas

In survival situations, a bag of frozen peas
can be used to strain water. Can be used as a glove,
a potholder, as a pouch or bandage, as a weapon
(if the peas are truly frozen), and as a pillow
when stuffed with socks, grass,
or leaves.

You can use a bag of frozen peas
to store drinking water. It is a great vessel,
a floatation device and slingshot, a tourniquet
for the spirit.

You can use it to signal help, the shiny parts
of the bag reflecting so well that airplanes
100 miles away will see it.
If you fashion your confusion into a hook,
you can also lure fish with the peas.

There are scenarios where a bag of frozen peas
can serve as a splint for minor injuries,
as an antenna for small electronics,
as a fingernail cleaner or compass.

A bag of frozen peas is strong enough to bind, build,
snare, and stitch, and generally make amends.

If you lose your eye, a bag of frozen peas
can be an eye patch. If you lose your way, it can mark
trails. If you hold the bag of frozen peas
until your thighs smolder, it will help you concentrate.

II: Mountain Goats…

Ten Poems on Marriage plus a Wish

I.

Victoria's Secret's models: what do they
write about? What models do supermodels model
their confidence on? Does anyone still read

the leaves in their tea? When you're having lunch,
listening to that Men at Work song
about the vegemite sandwich while thinking

of the zombie apocalypse, what's the Latin phrase
for that? What's the phrase for the songbird
that sounds berserk all through the baby's nap?

II.

When the snare I set snags
J & lifts her like a vision—
she must have known

when she said, *I do.*
Lord knows I did—
sort of. We weigh
the rules: trespassers for instance,
should they be shot on sight?
If we feel guilty
we know it's only in our heads,

like pleasure. We know
marriage is a body, & that a body
needs pain.

III.

The used-car salesman and finance manager
sit quietly in the next room. They think
we were born yesterday. They're listening in
on J and me as we express
our used-car reservations.
It gives us an opportunity: for J to say,
I love you, *but I think we should see other people.*
For me to say, *I'm pretty sure the condom broke;*
I think I'm pregnant again. To have never been
in this situation—eavesdropped upon
by untrustworthy used-car salesmen
while you wonder aloud with the one you love
if the minivan comes with guns and drugs—

IV.

Sometimes I try paying with knowledge. Like I'll toss

the diapers, wipes, and three cartons of cigarettes on
the counter; the teenage checkout girl
will give me a look and say, *57 dollars;*
and then I'll say, *I'm going to pay with knowledge.*

If she's brave, she'll look me in the eye
for as long as it takes. A kind of pleasure standoff...

That's usually when I confess I don't even smoke.
Never have.

V.

J behaving rationally, is there anything
more selfish? Hasn't she read these incoherent
instructions? Can't she see how powerless I am
against the screws gone missing from the box?
How much it hurts having to build this end table?

In my dreams, something else, an infinite column
of end tables endlessly collapsing.

VI.

We begin with the bills we most despise—
The membership at the vaguely Christian health club
           where our gear was stolen.

           Student loans to companies that harass us
for having been students who needed loans.
           Credit cards, electricity, water, alligator

                    wrestling lessons . . .

VII.

We dress as religious fanatics
when we're ready for sex—
to evoke the proper fear,
for how much braver it makes
for tearing off our clothes. . . .

VIII.

I like a beer at noon.
I like sitting outside in summer
with friends drinking noontime beers.
I try not to ogle the pert waitress. . . .
I make a toast to youth. . . .
Then I go home & wait
for the end of the world.
I rush my confused family
into the basement.
Quiet, I say, *or we won't hear the flood.*
There's a flood? the kids say,
starting to cry.

Only if we're lucky. We have to believe.
If there are better ways to forge a tradition,
I'm all ears. . . .

IX.

I'll say something: *I too was once a crawfish.*
Never was I freer from sin! And my wife, like a great sea,

ignores it. This ignoring washes over me. It forms
the heart of things. It's how we keep the love alive!

X.

I bring the weed-whipper indoors.
I begin to weed-whip the couch and floors.
J screams, *Why? Why?*
Because we have to try, I say. *Because I feel old.*
A couple like us should have more friends. . . .
Knocking holes in plaster, removing screws
from a hinge—it takes courage.
This is what a marriage knows.

XI.

Surely you've been asked,
Of anyone dead or alive, whom would you invite to dinner?
I'd invite Jesus, of course.
I'd ask him, "How's your dad? What's up with my lawn?
Were you not technically a zombie? Why all the haters?
Why all the shame?"
Basically what I'm saying is this:
I'd invite Jesus over so I could bore him to death.

Mountain Goats

My roommates
were all named Matt.
The one who hogged the TV.
The narcoleptic kleptomaniac
and his weirdly religious brother
who sold pyramid schemes
from the trunk of a rusted Gremlin.
The one who went stargazing—

90 percent of the crap in the sink was his.
The one who came back one night
from the bars with a cracked rib
was like living with Godzilla.
The one who broke a cello.
The one who called Dubuque
a shitfuck of white people.
Matts and more Matts
like a clown car of roommates
who kept me up
with unintelligible debates—
The Bermuda Triangle
versus The Bermuda Parallelogram,

Jesus versus daddy issues.
Is earth just a flea
on a dog's tail? Are all waiting rooms
plots to ruin our lives?
I was afraid the Matts

could read my thoughts
when what I should have been afraid of since it
happened enough
was losing my share of rent
at the casino then throwing up

in an alley
or watching nature shows
high on pills—
Me and the Matts losing our minds
while some idiot pissed off a snake,
while up in the Andes amazing goats
balanced on impossible ledges
made impossible leaps.

Cold Caller

I pictured my money crashed through a windshield. I
pictured my money, landing square in a stranger's lap.
This was back in the '90s, when I was succeeding (all
the time) at being kind of terrible & confused. I didn't
want insurance. I wanted accidents. The gamble. To fuck
everything or kick from it the ever-loving shit. . . . That
need that makes us chase our tails.

But when the cold caller asked if I had insurance, my
thoughts were winged with a purplish glow. (I know; I was
on pills then too, to let the old spine sip its fluid.) So I let
her sing her song.

It felt personal, like gazing from a ledge. And I remember
my shoes were untied. So when I thanked the cold caller
she couldn't hear; I'd fuzzed up the apartment with radio
static. I'd dropped the phone so long ago to bend down
and tie my shoes.

3 a.m.

Try to stop the hamster wheel
        of worries but the world
is berserk, the Middle East is berserk
                Putin is Berserk and al-Assad
        ISIS Christian fundamentalist, county clerks
science books in Kansas

noxious invasive taproots in summer
        what we've done to the oceans
all the wasted food and itchy trigger fingers
        America and its loud obnoxious
                American-ness like a drunk horny muscle-
head frat boy on spring break
with daddy's 401K, our gun lust

and privilege, how we care more for it
        for The Cubs and Donald Trump's
                pinched lemon of a face
        than the body of a black kid

                        pulled over on his bike
        for not having a light.
When the cop says, "What's in the backpack?" and the kid says,
        "Why?" and the cop says,
                "We can do this here or at the station. . . ."

                        you bet the kid makes a run for it—
        we all know how this could end
and how do we explain it?
How to teach *my* kids not to be complicit?

To tip the scales when half the time
        all I want is a book and a beer
and a band on vinyl?

They've seen me lose it over a cat box
or a hole in the wall, never mind
        what's happening on the Southside
or in the idiot governor's mansion?

Then I hear the cat at the door.
He wants in
        to the cozy home
                —only 240 payments left!—
        wants a hot meal
        so he can get even fatter then crash
on my pillow, flick his tail in my face

                while upstairs our son shouts in his sleep.
        I hope it's a good dream he's having
                hope he's ruling the world
of Minecraft or kicking Donkey Kong's
        ass, not being menaced
                by larger abstractions or vaporized in a flash
like those *The Day After* nightmares
        I had when I was a kid, when Reagan
                smiled crocodile smiles
        and trickle-down economics was scarier
than Freddy. I need

                                        beauty sleep so
                                        I won't sleep
                                through the beauty. Or
                                should I nudge
                        my wife

        sing, "Get up, get up, get up, get up. . . ."
But it takes her forever to fall asleep

her own hamster wheel spinning
        American doubts.
Now that she's out snoring that sweet

soft snore, I know she's dreaming her way
for once to the other side of morning
        where this time, luckily, that kid
on the bike makes it home alive
        so he can come to class and hand me his essay
about how his grandmother taught him
to read. In the morning, the world

has to stretch, work out the kinks
        in its back and knees. Our kids bound
down the stairs and into our bed
        make fart jokes and pretend to be ghosts
        for hugs and cereal. For a minute
in our house and maybe in yours
        we are in it together—everything not OK
but OK—sitting around a table
eating spoonfuls of Life.

Roughneck Twine

The epic way I rolled out of bed this morning.
The thrilling, emotionally moving way
I went downstairs and fixed cereal for the kids.

It was all so intense. . . . It was all so complex. . . .
The way we brushed our teeth,
the way I kneeled at the tub and washed

my ridiculous hair. Whatever the great
philosophers ponder, surely it was there,
out in the yard, where the kids

had urged me on with sticks to witness
the action of the ripening berries, the deep-seeded
symbolism of the beans

planted weeks ago, now finally winding
with flair up the twine. The roughneck twine
strung on the villainous fence

of flawless one-liners. The no-holds-barred.
The pathos. The commando, die-
hard way I loaded the kids in the car

and aimed us towards the day. Big trouble
and little troubles. The stuff of experience
blowing up all around as I drove them to school.

Fathers

They spend trillions, in line at Mickey D's grabbing burgers
on the fly. They need to work on their baby talk, their *goochy goo*,
but they have other problems. Presidential problems. Problems with
   crossword puzzles.

Strangling the vacuum cleaner problems. Problems in the bathroom and
   problems in bed.
They say things no one wants to hear like, "Listen!" Like, "Don't touch
   that!"
Like, "Where's the bourbon? Where are my sweatpants?" They replace
   the thingy on things,

smear lipstick, forget dog food, buy mugs personalized with Calvin
   taking a piss
on common sense or "Never Trust an Atom, They Make Up Everything."
They slip into dreams of unlimited credit but the details slip away.

One out of three is a sitcom. Even more are confused. If you want
to be a good father, sing. Maybe mine did; I don't remember,
but when he came back from Vietnam he ended up on a corner

in San Francisco peddling flyers for the resistance. Now he's part Fox
   News Republican.
Part drastic measures. An episode, random escapades of extreme distance
   fathering.
He's not two gay dads; he's a testimony to Super Bowl ads.

Some stay at home, make you squint at their glaring flaws. America awash
in fathers who make their mothers and husbands and wives and
   girlfriends cry,
a strange centrifugal force, when they disconnect

from what they think or want, they flood themselves with guilt. From a
    window
in my memory I still see the scene, sepia-toned, my father with a suitcase
in each hand, my father in a jacket in a tie, my father leaving. I was
    four. . . .

They are an emotional performance, a myth. They spread the gospel
sometimes of Jesus, sometimes of huddling together nervously at the
    cliff's edge.
They are data points that rise and fall with mortgage rates. Data points
    that scatter

like insane plots. They have names like Tom or Stan or Michelle.
I wasn't raised by my father, and it surprises J still that I don't resent him
    for it. How can I?
We too have kids. We know how brutal it is. . . .

When my son was 2, I went to the gas station for emergency milk
then filled up the tank and thought—because I was exhausted,
because I was out of my fathering mind—I could drive 300 hundred miles
    right then.

Point the car north, floor it into Lake Superior and never come back.
Another tank I could even drive to the moon. My father thought that too.
It's why I'm able to love him.

Holland

You should write something
about tulips,
      my wife says. She's sitting up in bed
with her shirt off, the baby
on one of her tits. The vibrant colors, she says, reds
and purples, the mind-blowing blooms, those elegant
      cups like turbans on smooth
green stems. The baby for a moment
      stops sucking to fart. My wife farts. I join in.
My wife goes on: They're like
      something from a dream,
she says. They mimic lilies.
Live for hundreds of years. Cook up
      like onions. Triumph. Darwins. Swan
Wings. Rembrandts. They can mean almost anything.
      Now the baby has stopped sucking altogether.
Her eyes roll back in her head. I peel
      off my shorts to air
the sweat from my crotch. Okay,
I say. And what
      would we call this thing?
My wife considers
this for a moment. Then says, thoughtfully,
      How about Fat Loads
of Hot Salty Jizz?

The Brood Stock

A commercial for yogurt or something, it doesn't really matter, it's just sexy people standing around smiling, soaking in the celestial light, sounding like they're about to come.

I fall off my barstool.

I walk to the river, where small, mysterious fish pucker the surface with their tiny mouths.

The brood-stock, slow-finning in the shallows—I wade out, am about to snag one with my bare hands when I notice sprouting from its back fins the pinkish stubs of tiny human legs.

Illegitimate Daughters

When my wife and I considered a move
to Terre Haute—
it doesn't matter now why; it never happened—
a friend of mine, though,
said cost of living-wise, it was tough to beat.

He also said his dad, who still lived there,
would take me musky fishing,
and that musky fishing involved something
called *double cowgirls*, which sounded amazing,
like a sex position, or a terrible movie,
or a theory.

Otherwise The Haute
(that's what my friend called it) was balls.

I wondered about that—
balls good or bad?—
but instead of asking I sent a text
that went like this: *whose balls are these,*
I think I know . . .
And my friend texted back: *but his taint*
is in the village though . . .

Then I Googled "Terre Haute"
and found out it's French for "highland."
But that wasn't what my friend had said at all.
He had said something more beautiful.
He had said "Terre Haute" was Hoosier
for how easy it was
to spot Larry Bird's illegitimate daughters.

The Kalevala

The Kalevala is awesomely about *sisu* and saunas and Nokia phones.
It shows how Finland just hatched one morning from an egg. Reading it

makes you feel like your muscles are thinking, like you're smashing windows
with a stag's antlers. Like you're listening to every one of Iron Maiden's albums

at once. It makes *me* wish I was more than a quarter Finn. It makes me wish
I was five-quarter Finn and staring at the sea saying, by Ukko, god of thunder

and sky, the fucking sea! *The Kalevala* turns Santa
into a sledgehammer. It inspired all of Finland's great rally drivers

who can pretty much can drink us under the table. There's a cycle called
"Kicking Russia's Ass Again!" but Russia's ministers don't care.

They're too busy with mistresses who take off their boots to punish them
with the sweat from their soles. They're too busy being foot slaves. *The Kalevala*

pretty much explains how an ex-boy-or-girlfriend can just come over, take off
their clothes, and trash your apartment. Then a bunch of Finns
give a bear a bear-hug and the funeral's the next day. One time
when I lost my copy, the copy found me. It threatened to put me in the hospital

if that ever happened again. Then it called up the Captain
and said please bring me my wine. And then—get this—the Captain said

we haven't had that spirit here since 1835 when the First Edition
was published. After that an oak tree catches fire and some reindeer
    thunder

through a meadow, which I never understand. But sometimes not
    understanding
is the best answer. *The Kalevala* taught me that.

7-11

Life's too short for munchies at 7-11
to cost double and triple. Thus the cashier—

who's been there too long, who's dealt
with a thousand rude customers tonight alone
and knows you don't have forever,

      what with that anxious look on your face
and the hour—
                        thus the cashier asks
if you would like beer with that
as she slides the condoms across the counter.

You count out exact change but it doesn't matter.
Back at the apartment,
      some dude on the first floor
who loves mayonnaise sandwiches
      puts the final touches
on a paint-by-numbers *Mona Lisa;*

                        down the hall
some kids into death metal and ratty Chuck Taylors
discover a mother's stash;

      and out beneath the parking lot lights
a genius working on a muscle car
                has totally killed the mood.

Your lover—who's wearing only
      your Iron Maiden t-shirt, who's just fine
by herself reading a magazine,
who's trying to figure out
                how she wants this to end—

is awake.

III: Dear Kids...

Static

I cheated on every girlfriend. Was pistol-whipped
in an alley by a jealous lover. Watched porn
on my cellphone. Shot the windshield
out of a neighbor's car when I was drunk. Crushed
pills on a sink: Oxy, Soma, Ecstasy, Vicodin,
Codeine, Percocet. When I felt outside myself,
life would unfold from a distance. My father
was a soldier, my mother lonely all her life. She said
they should all be shot, right-wing conservatives
and religious freaks. I have delusions of adequacy.
I do not believe in God. Whenever I think,
I quickly meet the limits of my thinking.
When I was tempted to regrets—
my life, my wife, and my children whom I love
and who love me back—
shame filled me with a religious intensity.

Because I wanted something. Or something else.
And still these dreams: of my mother looking out
from my reflection, of hospital beds in a mirror.
If I blink, I'm afraid you'll disappear. In the '80s,
in my hillbilly hometown, I had a mullet;
that's one example. There's no word that leaves
the self behind. Food stamps from time to time;
clothes from Salvation Army. I thought language
would save me or make me richer, not point back
at what I've tried to outrun. I tried.
Didn't want to work at the gun factory,
didn't want to work in the mill like my brother,
scrubbing tanks so filthy our mother
had to hose him off in the drive. To feel alive.
To feel more than this feeling of feeling around
for something to feel. The inner work ongoing.
I am a northerner. My father wanted me

to be an architect. My mother took no shit.
So I went to the movies high, went to the diner high;
the eggs on my plate seemed to watch me.
Spent a night in jail. Then another. When I found my
neighbor's body, I was afraid. She was old,
had been dead for days. I couldn't speak clearly, and
wish now I hadn't called the cops right away. Wish
I'd gone through her things to see
what was left behind. Even now, there are secrets
I keep even from myself. I know damn well
what that makes me.

Civil Disobedience

Thoreau never saw those YouTube videos of African Guinea worms, erupting from a blister on some poor fucker's foot to puke kids into the gleaming world.

When the worms chewed through Thoreau, they probably tasted big ideas. They probably tasted chicken, which tastes like civil disobedience.

Thoreau got all the credit for roughing it like the first hippie, but while he wandered the woods drinking tallboys of PBR, his mom did all his laundry.

He thought it was so sublime, that bug at the end of *Walden* chewing free from a table that had sat in some farmer's kitchen for a thousand years.

Thoreau was probably a pervert. He should have wandered out to the mall, talked dirty to the raccoons rummaging the rubbage bins. He should have checked out that movie *Alien*. That scene where the space bug in John Hurt's spaghetti stomach bursts and scoots its laundry of gore past the horrified crew. That transcendental scene I'd love to see Thoreau seeing for the first time. For the look on his face; that beautiful sublime.

Upon Turning 40

I blamed a bag snagged (and thrashing)
in a fence for making me think, "What a bird!"
I sang along to that Bowie song, "Clown control
to Mao Zedong." Said with confidence,
the possum's not playing; he's passed out
from terror. Googled sleep remedies
and got instructions for how to date a mermaid.
Right there, on my phone. Later, when someone
said, "Don't get me started on the Dead Kennedys,"
suddenly I remembered that time
I accidentally wrote on a resume, "References
will be furnaced upon request." Some mistakes
are perfect; some make way more sense.

The Day Some Plumbing Died

It's 5:40 a.m. on a Sunday, already it has us in its throat, our son trying to harness the cat, trying to trap it in laundry baskets, trying to make it wear socks, then our daughter with a tummy ache, it's what she says when she's hungry, she wants Cheerios, wants Cheerios *now*, though not Cheerios that are brown or tan, not Cheerios that look like Cheerios, Cheerios that taste like something else, so okay honey

Give me a minute while my body makes these hurting sounds (not hung-over exactly, just feeling squishy) and when I step on a block it cramps up my foot so it drags like an anchor, all I want is to spray-paint every wall in the house—*I don't want a fucking tie for Father's Day! I don't want fucking soap on a rope!*—all I want is to be the meatloaf hiding out in the fridge, to not have to scoop unburied cat turds big enough to belong to a horse

And while the kids fight again over a roll of tape or something sparkly-eyed and pink, over a song my son sings but he swears not at his sister, while everyone fights for attention I get it and feel like I'm failing the test, feel like I'm driving through the drive-thru in reverse as my wife with dazzle and grace makes her way to the kitchen to make the best coffee

Then I wonder what she's thinking, wonder if paradise is a secret that slowly tears you apart while off in the distance we still have friends who stay up late drinking bourbon, playing video games, blasting the Pixies on vinyl and in a few hours, when the water finally seeps through the closet, I'll have to call a plumber

About a pipe in the ceiling that's been leaking money for weeks, but that hasn't happened yet, I'm still unaware sitting there on the couch drinking coffee with my wife, listening to our kids list all the things they'd like to flush down the toilet, lightning, a castle, zombies, and chicken butts, and I say wait, what, but it's too late, they've moved on laughing, doing this feel-better dance that requires devotion.

Sex Toy

—after years of marriage

Some of it made sense; the air pedals
wired to the head clamps, for instance. The spindle

that had to be waxed after every turn.
But the inflatable unicorn gave way to concerns.

And how were we to run the extenulator
to experience the bliss of the fribbets

without a commercial license? How would we juice
the spangler without alerting the cops?

The sex toy's warnings glowed in the dark—
do not use near an open flame, may cause vertigo,

should not be inserted backwards. Then my wife
plugged the lithinodes into the sleeve;

the sex toy danced aggressively on the dresser
with little regard for safety or space.

It challenged the thought
of a self altogether. "What the hell

are you talking about?" my wife said. Experiments
that discover pleasure strip language to a moan.

Thankfully we still don't know all its settings.

Someone Has to Make a List

Call the contractors and not get
bullied into saying yes. Someone
has to drag the push-mower
back to the shed before
it rains, before rust ruins its blades.
Someone has to go into the yard
and rave, shirtless and un-
showered, at the cats
who mean
to shit in the
garden.
Someone
has to sandblast dried
sauce
from the plates. Plant beans.
Make
sure everyone has at
least
one thing. Someone has to find
the cards missing from the board
game, locate the princess flip-
flops, read Dr. Seuss over and over
no matter how blue or red.
Someone has to give high-fives
and say hello, wipe the spilled
milk before it congeals, before the table
becomes a milky stamp.
Someone has to collect the stray
mini-wheats
beneath the
bed.

Someone has to love this,
has to make oatmeal (clothing optional),
has to go down to the basement
and throw it all away: the
molding

Bankers Boxes full of
memories,
the files and
instructions to
who-
knows-what, out-of-style
shorts
and shirts, books and books

and books but definitely not
the guitar that needs new strings
and pegs and definitely not
the drums. Someone has to assume,
has to resonate, has to find
where the remote is buried in the un-
vacuumed couch, which means
someone has to vacuum
the cushions, which means
someone
first must borrow
or buy
a vacuum.
Someone
must be
sure,
be vigilant with
leftovers,
be certain no sugar
sweetens
the counters lest the ants
start marching. Someone has to flower,
has to measure and simmer
and bundle and sweep, adjust the antenna,
turn it all on and off and on again
without crying, but why does it
have to be me?

"Just You and the Open Road"

—after an email from Airbnb

> just you and the open road and the heavy you are not alone >
    just you
and the open road and a blow-up doll in a ditch
    never mind > everything's fine

> just you and the song and the open road and Fascist
    gas-bags on the radio > crackpots at rest stops > quarter-thieving
machines vending bad medicine > some stone-age
    epitaph inked over a smiley face in a stall you try to blossom
out with toilet paper and spit > just you and the open road

    which is a drug > a room that needs cleaning > a stray sock
and shoe in the median > gods dwindling
    in the twilight > acres and acres of transgenic crops
murmuring like a heart > like paranoia but at least you're there

    > just you and the open air through a free
country if you never mind its incarceration rates > never mind
  landscapes
    pocked with Taco Bells and McDonald's
where they may as well pay in food stamps or salt > diapers that last 500
  years >
    Wal-Marts the size of Parthenons troubling every direction >

just you and the open road and symphonic
    static through states where the highest paid officials
are football coaches > you and the open road and your heart and
  obligations tonight >
    3,000 gun shows a year > hormones > billboards for strippers in
      the suburbs
> xenophobic preachers hating from here to Hell
    Michigan > tick tock >

just you and the open road where frankly it's not linguistics
> not William Blake or lambs > it's a NASCAR race > not
everyone
pulls over before they text or dance or eat soup
or get busy or Facebook cat videos >

just you and the open road and love > 1.4 billion
pounds of trash daily > 100 million orphans > satellites
jellied with lasers > all the space in the world
for you to become while some president boils in need
of psychotherapy and meds >

just you and the open road and pleasure and the money you dropped
on childcare and Kraft dinners and loans >
spreadsheets and to-do lists chopping
through your thoughts à la Nicholson in *The Shining*
> but don't fool yourself > if it's a three-day weekend > say it's
Labor Day
> say the radio is drunk with Bowie and Prince
and Leonard Cohen > say the person next to you is ready to talk
fear >
ready to talk infidelity and desire so something real
can reach in > maybe then > maybe there's time <

Nostalgia

Remember dying of dysentery on the Oregon Trail?
Remember when your mom said, Shut up and eat your
dinner?

Could we please quit pretending we miss cassette tapes?
That there are things when there are only half things?

Nostalgia is for idiots, my mother would say, crying at baby
pictures. Nostalgia is for crotchety old goats that miss the
pickpockets in Times Square.

Meanwhile, on a good night, you can see for quadrillions
of miles, all the way back to the first comedy and the first
double-dare.

What do you remember from 1989?

I remember my ridiculous friend's unreliable Plymouth
Reliant. I remember saying no to *Just Say No* and Nancy
Reagan's freakish head. I remember finding horror in *The
Joy of Sex* under my mother's bed.

If I ever get another pet rock, I won't name it Rocky. When
I stare into the imperfect vacuum of outer space, I won't
get sentimental for the good old days, when vacuum repair
salesmen went door-to-door.

Adjustable Beds

We're in hospital beds on an empty stage,
my bare feet sticking out from the covers,
my mother (dead now 10+ years)
in the next bed over (sitting upright
in her adjustable bed), dressed like a nurse,
an IV infusing her with a silvery light.
When the curtain rises, it's not on an audience
or an empty auditorium but the cosmos itself.
A deep space of stars, swirling galaxies.
My mother smiles. She has this look.
"See?" she says. "I told you."

Transverse

Wear a tutu
       or get poison sumac just once
and everyone
          remembers
the look on your face. If the password
             is *Sue saw seven sleek seals*
      it's a good time
         I hope you remember.
I remember
      my mother loved lilacs best,
          the cockatiel
      she trained to say,

Here, kitty kitty. When darkness settles,
     deeper beauty illumines,
     memorized in the stained glass. After a few
     minutes, boiling
        water remembers
     the dumplings
        to float like a thought.
     If you remember *Your ass is grass*,
maybe you and I are related. She smiled
     saying it was like lovers
         the way the cats
         would spat

with the jays. If they say
         the premise
      is simple, there's probably a thing or two
    they forgot. Maybe not.
            Maybe, my mother said. *I swear to God.*
       Reaching down with both hands
           to grab my shoulders
           in a dream.

She could remember nothing
        like it, the government
               just giving her
      money for being sick. From
           the stone age of mix-tapes you remember

       yesterday walking hand in hand
          or a faded sign
          by the side of the road saying 15 miles

to the love shack. Not being the brightest crayon
       in the box
           is inevitable,
lest we ever forget.
       Will I ever forget seeing her
get thinner and weak?
           I remember ideas
              and sensations,

said Joyce, pretty much speaking
       for everyone.
By the time you remember
       you have to swim back,
         your legs should feel like jello. There is no shore.
There is no
swimming back.
Mother, I remember your face.

Substitute

A small plastic goat had been left on the desk. I let it graze the notes overhead where it amplified to goat-size. "A goat-sized goat," I said. "Write it down. In a field of words thick as soda cans." There were looks of concern. The muscle relaxers I'd taken were starting to kick in. I flicked the projector's negative switch & messed with its iris.

I had no idea what I was doing—I'm sure the students could tell—but it made an interesting x-ray effect so I went with it. "Note the plum-colored void," I said. "That's where bitterness and trouble go." A smiling kid in the front (he'd been clowning around) finally fell back in his chair. What a lesson, I thought. With the teeth of a goat. I couldn't wait to share it.

Dear Kids

I get nostalgic for summer, for hair bands
on the radio, songs about beer and girls, the terrible
"Every Rose Has Its Thorn" and "Wanted Dead or Alive."
I find a line from Yeats—
In wise love each divines the high secret self of the other—
and wonder how to use it on your mother,
wonder how metaphysics can get me
out of doing dishes. I never said I was perfect.
Meanwhile, in the food court where time
tries to kill us, the teenagers look like music
video druid queens, and when the skate punks
start with the dick jokes, we move
to another table. One day I'll try to explain it,
the weirdos and White McFlight, the Taco Bell blight
and the holes in my wallet. I'll have to explain
tragedy without falling down a sewer hole.
I'll have to explain the red face of guilt
when what I want is to not lose my hair.
What did you expect? Pokémon forever?
A daddy with no issues? In our day we played
hide and seek while church gave God
nightmares about us and school gave us
feelings about planets and grades.
Then they kicked Pluto out like an old pair of shoes.
Even now I'm totally clueless; I don't want a tie
for Father's Day, dammit, and beneath the glossy sheen,
White Lion and Dokken were real.
When those whales washed up on the beach
in the news, you were sad but I said look,
it's something, all those strangers gathered
with buckets urging the beasts to swim. Dear kids,
I felt the weight of love, then folded up
a blank piece of paper and tucked it under
your mother's pillow. How else can I say it?
All I want is for you to be fuel
for your own beautiful machines.

Acknowledgments

Thank you to the following journals, where versions of these poems originally appeared.

"Illegitimate Daughters" in *Ampersand Review*
"Ten Poems on Marriage plus a Wish" in *Anti-*
"Civil Disobedience" in *Barn Owl Review*
"'Just You and the Open Road'" in *Blue Earth Review*
"Fathers" in *Columbia Poetry Review*
"Mountain Goats" in *Crab Creek Review*
"Holland" in *Forklift*
"Un-Buddha" in *Jet Fuel Review*
"*The Kalevala*" in *Pleiades*
"Transverse" in *Sou'wester*
"Sex Toy" in *TYPO*
"A Late-Night Conversation with My Infant Son in a Convenience Store
    Parking Lot" in *Watershed*

"Bastille Day," "Totally Doable," "Ten Poems on Marriage plus a Wish,"
"Holland," "The Brood Stock," "Illegitimate Daughters," "Civil Disobedience,"
"Sex Toy," and "Substitute" appear in the chapbook Civil Disobedience (Rabbit
Catastrophe Press, 2017)

To my students, for the gifts of humor and light.

To my Saluki brethren and especially my teachers Rodney Jones, Allison
Joseph, and the late Lucia Perillo: you have my endless gratitude.

To Mary Biddinger, Amy Freels, and everyone at the University of Akron
Press: thank you for your faith, support, and careful attention.

To those friends and writers whose work inspires me, especially Adam Fell,
Matt Hart, Kara Candito, Erika Meitner, Sandra Simonds, Adrian Matejka,

Josh Bell, Bruce Cohen, Emilia Philips, Michael Theune, Ron Mitchell, Aimee Nezhukumatathil, Brett Ralph, Jennifer Militello, Traci Brimhall, Adam Clay, Ryan Collins, Ryan Browne, and Rita Mae Reese.

To Julie and our beautiful children August and Josie: your forgiveness and love move these poems.

For my brothers. For my father, Philip Gerard Guenette (1946–2017).

Photo: Aliza Rand

Matthew Guenette received an MFA from Southern Illinois University. He is the author of two previous poetry collections: *American Busboy* (University of Akron Press, 2011) and *Sudden Anthem* (Dream Horse Press, 2008) as well as a chapbook, *Civil Disobedience* (Rabbit Catastrophe Press, 2017). Recent work has appeared in *Forklift, Ohio*; *Spoon River Poetry Review*; *Sou'wester*; *Southern Indiana Review*; and *TYPO*. He lives in Madison, Wisconsin, and teaches composition and creative writing at Madison College.